SPOT
FEELINGS

JEALOUS

by Rachel Bach

arms crossed   cry

Look for these words and pictures as you read.

pout   look away

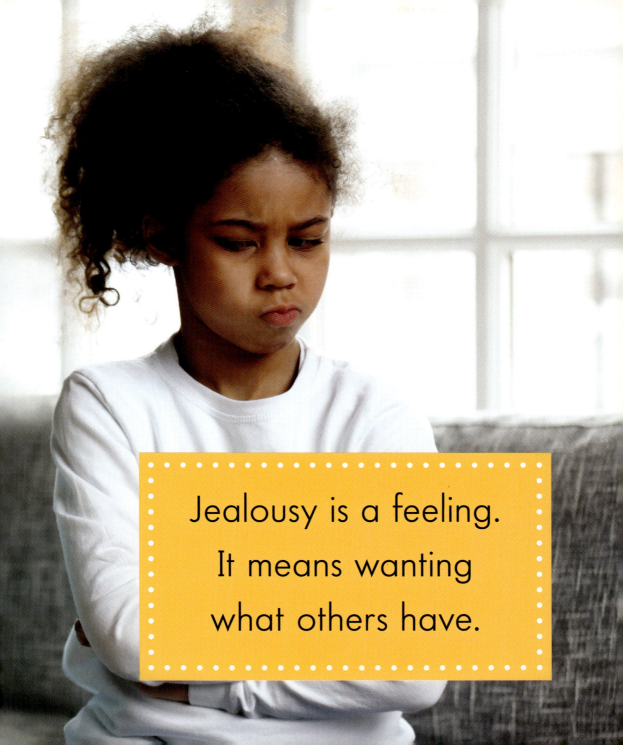

Jealousy is a feeling. It means wanting what others have.

Lily is jealous.
Her friend got candy.
She pouts.

pout

arms crossed

Omar's brother scores a goal.
Omar does not cheer.
He is jealous.
He crosses his arms.

look away

Emma has a younger brother. Her dad spends more time with him. Emma feels alone. She looks away.

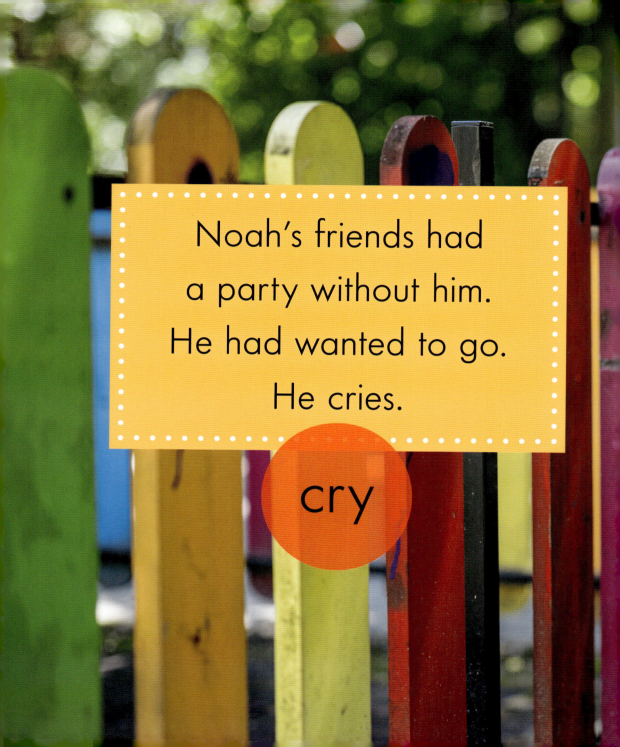

Noah's friends had a party without him. He had wanted to go. He cries.

cry

It is normal to feel jealous. Talk with a grown-up.

What makes you jealous?

arms crossed   cry

Did you find?

pout   look away

Spot is published by Amicus Learning, an imprint of Amicus
P.O. Box 227, Mankato, MN 56002
www.amicuspublishing.us

Copyright © 2025 Amicus.
International copyright reserved in all countries.
No part of this book may be reproduced in any form without written permission from the publisher.

Library of Congress Cataloging-in-Publication Data
Names: Bach, Rachel, author.
Title: Jealous / by Rachel Bach.
Description: Mankato, MN : Amicus Learning, [2025] | Series: Spot feelings | Audience: Ages 4–7 | Audience: Grades K-1 | Summary: "What makes kids feel jealous? Encourage social-emotional learning with this beginning reader that introduces vocabulary for discussing feelings of jealousy with an engaging search-and-find feature"—Provided by publisher.
Identifiers: LCCN 2024017557 (print) | LCCN 2024017558 (ebook) | ISBN 9798892000819 (library binding) | ISBN 9798892001397 (paperback) | ISBN 9798892001977 (ebook)
Subjects: LCSH: Jealousy in children—Juvenile literature. | Jealousy—Juvenile literature.
Classification: LCC BF723.J4 B33 2025 (print) | LCC BF723.J4 (ebook) | DDC 152.4/8—dc23/eng/20240502
LC record available at https://lccn.loc.gov/2023039320
LC ebook record available at https://lccn.loc.gov/2023039321

Printed in China

Ana Brauer, editor
Deb Miner, series designer
Kim Pfeffer, book designer and photo researcher

Photos by Dreamstime/Prostockstudio, 12–13; Freepik/freepik, 4–5; Getty Images/Mixmike, 10–11; Shutterstock/fizkes, 3, juan carlos tinjaca, 1, Lopolo, cover, nazarovsergey, 4–5, pixelheadphoto digitalskillet, 14, Tatyana Dzemileva, 8–9, wavebreakmedia, 6–7